LEARN TO DRAW

Disney PRINCESS
palace pets

Walter Foster Jr.

Printed in Shenzhen, China, January 2015
1 3 5 7 9 10 8 6 4 2
19057

Table of Contents

Tools & Materials

You only need a few art supplies to create all of your favorite Palace Pets. Start with a drawing pencil, and have a pencil sharpener and an eraser nearby. When you've finished drawing, you can add color with markers, colored pencils, or paint. It's up to you!

drawing pencil & paper

sharpener

eraser

colored pencils

felt-tip markers

paintbrushes & paints

How to Use This Book

In this book you'll learn to draw all of your favorite Palace Pets in just a few simple steps. With a little practice, you'll soon be able to create new drawings of your own!

1

First draw the basic shapes, using light lines that are easy to erase.

2

Each new step is shown in blue, so you know what to draw next.

3

Follow the blue lines to draw the details.

4

Now darken the lines you want to keep, and erase the rest.

5

Use some Princess sparkle (crayons and markers) to add color to your drawing!

Pumpkin & Bibbidy

One starry night, Cinderella stepped out onto her palace balcony and found Pumpkin, an adorable silky white puppy. Cinderella was even more surprised to discover that the precious puppy was an anniversary present from Prince Charming! Pumpkin always looks glamorous in her sparkling tiara. She loves to attend royal balls, and when the orchestra starts playing, she twirls and dances on her hind legs with the grace of a princess. Bibbidy is the most helpful pony in the palace stables, and she adores doing chores and helping Cinderella plan royal balls.

Pumpkin

1

2

3

4

Bibbidy

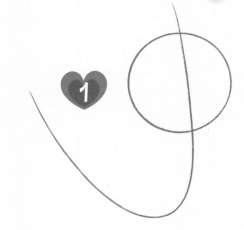

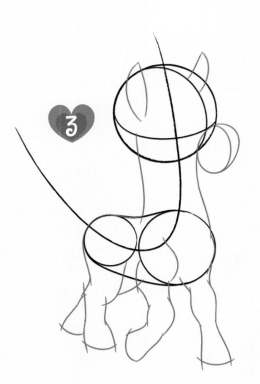

Beauty & Bloom

Since the day Aurora found Beauty sleeping in the palace garden, they've been inseparable. This graceful kitten adores sleeping. She even has a little mask that she uses to help her doze during the day! Day or night, you'll often find her cuddled up with Aurora, smelling of sweet rose perfume. Bloom, a charming pink pony with a purple mane and tail, loves to be showered with attention. She was a gift from Prince Phillip, and Aurora loves spending time with her!

Beauty

Bloom

Teacup & Petite

Teacup is an outgoing puppy with a love for attention. She first caught Belle's eye in the village square while she was performing for the villagers. Teacup has a great sense of style, and she always chooses the perfect accessories for any occasion. Petite is Belle's beautiful and adventurous pony. Like Belle, Petite loves to explore, but sometimes her daring personality gets the best of her.

Teacup

Petite

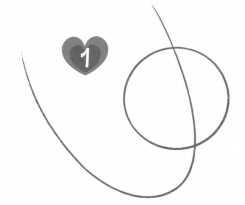

1

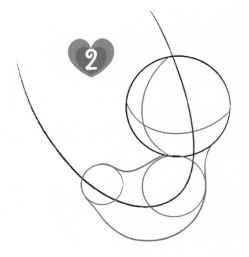

2

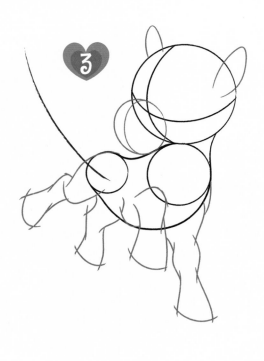

3

4

Treasure & Seashell

Prince Eric found Treasure, a curious and playful kitten with a love for adventure, during a sea voyage, and Ariel fell in love with her immediately. The two are a perfect pair—they both adore swimming and have luxurious red hair that smells like the freshest sea breeze. Ariel's endearing purple pony, Seashell, also has a long, flowing red mane and tail. Seashell is a little clumsy, but she has a heart of gold and loves living on land.

Treasure

Seashell

Berry & Sweetie

During a stroll in the forest, Snow White discovered Berry hiding beneath a blueberry bush, eating all of the delicious berries she could find. Berry is a shy bunny with soft fur and a fluffy white tail. Sweetie is the perfect name for Snow White's delightful pony. Her genuine, loving nature and cheerful personality endear her to everyone she meets. She loves to help Snow White make delicious pies—but she loves to eat them more!

Berry

Sweetie

1

2

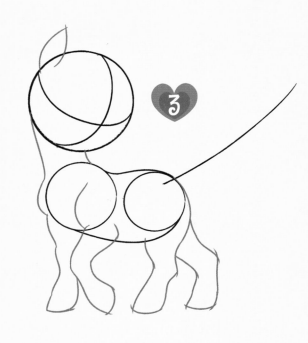

3

4

Blondie, Summer, Daisy & Meadow

A guard horse has to be brave and loyal. Blondie is both of these things—but she's also very sweet! Rapunzel noticed her right away among the royal horses on the day of her welcome home parade. Summer is an outdoorsy kitten with a special talent for climbing trees. At first Summer was matted and dirty, but she just needed a little pampering at the Royal Beauty Salon. Daisy, an energetic puppy with a love for nature and playing outdoors, is a perfect match for Rapunzel, and her enthusiasm is contagious! Meadow is a friendly purple skunk with all of the elegance and grace necessary to make her the perfect royal companion.

Blondie

Summer

Daisy

1

2

3

4

Meadow

Lily & Bayou

In New Orleans, nothing is more important than good food and jazz music. Lily, Tiana's independent kitten, loves jazz and adores dressing up in her finest ragtime outfit. Bayou, an easygoing purple-haired pony, also loves dressing up for parades and celebrations. A gift from Prince Naveen's family, Bayou holds a special place in Princess Tiana's heart.

Lily

1

2

3

4

Bayou

Sultan

Jasmine found Sultan napping on a pile of precious silks at the market. As soon as she laid eyes on the tiny tiger, she knew that he was meant to live with her in the palace. Sultan is a strong, independent cub who has always wished for a family of his own to guard and protect. He has what it takes to be a perfect companion and lifelong friend to Jasmine. Sultan may be small, but his bravery is a million times his size!

Sultan

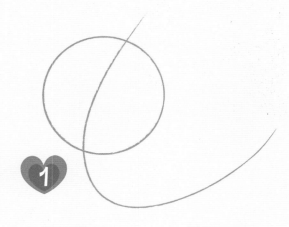

Windflower

Windflower is a playful, mischievous raccoon that is dear to Pocahontas's heart. Never straying too far from the princess, Windflower loves to have her big, fluffy tail brushed. Her curious personality and good-natured pranks always make Pocahontas smile. Windflower's adventurous spirit knows no bounds, and she is always eager to explore and make new friends.

Windflower

1

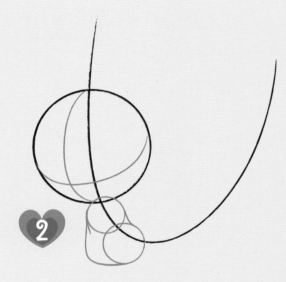

2

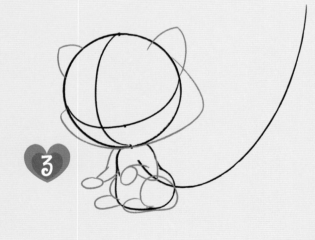

3

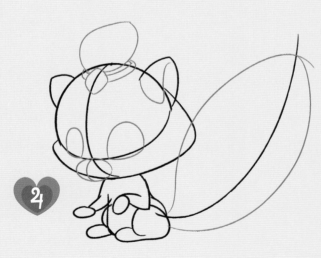

4

Blossom

Blossom is the most cheerful pet one could wish for. Mulan met her during a banquet, where she found the lovely panda hiding under her table snacking on all of the delicious food she could get her paws on! Blossom is a sweet and huggable bear with a gentle and loving personality. She is a constant and loyal friend to Mulan, and she loves her for who she is inside—a brave and kind daughter and friend, and a true hero!

Blossom

1

2

3

4